SWING
LOW
The Unexpected JESUS Appears

by

JUDY CHATHAM

Judy Chatham / Author's Tranquility Press
3900 N Commerce Dr. Suite 300 #1255
Atlanta, GA 30344
www.authorstranquilitypress.com

Ordering Information:
Quantity sales. Special discounts are available on quantity purchases by corporations, associations, and others. For details, contact the "Special Sales Department" at the address above.

Swing Low / Judy Chatham
Hardback: 978-1-964362-65-6
Paperback: 978-1-964362-15-1
eBook: 978-1-964362-16-8

**In Memory of
Mother Eunice McCart**

I am particularly indebted to the Rev. Patrick Sinnott of Orleans, Indiana, for it was his ministry to Mother and his Sunday sermon that introduced me to Luke 7:11-17.

Also, a special thanks to the staff at the Artist Colony in Nashville, Indiana for providing the perfect atmosphere for my writing. The late artists would have appreciated my efforts.

In a few cases in this manuscript, some names of persons and places were changed to protect their identity. Also, the situations described in this book are told as the author remembers them or interpreted them.

Table of Contents

Story #3

HE MADE THINGS RIGHT WITH MRS. GEORGES' TEA SET AND MORE

Story #4

HE SHOWED ME WHO I AM TO HIM

Story # 5

HE DROVE ME TO SCHOOL AND TAUGHT MY CLASS

Story # 6

HE ACCOMPLISHED HIS WORK WITHOUT ME

Story #7

HE USED HARRY EMERSON FOSDICK TO CONSOLE ME

Story # 8

HE ANSWERED PRAYERS PRAYED BY THE MOTHER SEVEN YEARS BEFORE HER DEATH

INTRODUCTION

Here's a special song. Jesus is coming into town, and may be walking directly into a reader's life with all of its mix of newly dscovered trouble and happy times. (As in Luke 7:7-11)

SWING LOW, SWEET CHARIOT

"The chariots of God are tens of thousands."

–Psalm 68:17

Words and music: African American spiritual

First recorded in 1909 by the Fisk Jubilee Singers

Refrain

Swing low, sweet chariot,

Coming for to carry me home,

Swing low, sweet chariot,

Coming for to carry me home.

I looked over Jordan, and what did I see?

Coming for to carry me home,

A band of angels coming after me,

Coming for to carry me home.

Refrain

If you get there before I do,

Coming for to carry me home,

Tell all my friends I'm coming too,

Coming for to carry me home.

Refrain

I'm sometimes up and sometimes down,

Coming for to carry me home,

But still my soul feels heavenly bound,

Coming for to carry me home.

Refrain

The brightest day that I can say,

Coming for to carry me home,

When Jesus washed my sins away,

Coming for to carry me home.

Refrain

For over a century and in the oral tradition before, people have found a common language in the singing of "Swing Low Sweet Chariot, Comin' for to carry me home." For decades I thought that "Swinging Low" was a one-time thing, when the angels came to carry us home to heaven. Now I see it as a multi-faceted experience that takes place over time. While at once our souls are saved upon accepting Jesus as the only way to have eternal salvation, our faith is built in stages.

Striving, Turning, and Finding appear to be the three steps to our deliverance in the Christian life. I see these as three parts to coming into a strong faith that says God is going to do what He said He would. For many the season of striving is long and delays the turning and finding.

In this discussion I have included my view of being a young convert in the Army of God spending many years of striving; then I have shown the flip side of that picture with what another member of the same Army did in only a few years of striving.

Finally I have added thirteen faith builder stories, each representing a stage, a rung on the ladder to a stronger faith. After all and through it all, the members of the Army of God desire to move on up in trust and faith in the approaching Jesus.

In the midst of all striving, help is on the way when a person has enlisted in the Army of God. Fortunately this is true for the newest convert as well as for the more mature one. We know this because one of the best "swing low" stories of the Bible surely must be our focus here: Luke 7:7-11.

When I was a freshman in high school, baton twirling fascinated me. With all kinds of lofty ideas of what a baton twirler's life's role is, I applied to be one of this high-stepping group. I had marched to the tune of "Onward Christian Soldiers" and knew that the person in the lead held the banner high and gave the signals for the marching troops to follow, to turn, or to go straight ahead. This baton corps should be the group for me.

I believe my view of life as a baton twirler came from what I had seen on the football field in the neighboring county. Into this larger school came a drum major for whom God had given an unusually flexible joint in his spine. Eddie would appear at the south end of the football field, tall, lean, in his English-Royal Guard-to-the-Queen fuzzy, fat and tall hat with the red feathered plume resting on top, his perfectly pressed uniform, his brass baton resting at his side. A slight breeze would be blowing his red plume, feathers stirring as in "rallying the troops for the mighty Achilles, or perhaps the mighty Hector." All would be quiet for what seemed like miles around. Street traffic provided a slight break in the silence, but that distant buzz of noise was all we heard. When Eddie took the field, everyone snapped to attention.

While Eddie had stood stone still since he first appeared, the band, on command, had been at ease. Then he blew his whistle and with total grace, his waist bent back so that his rustling red plume slightly brushed the sod of the ground behind him. Then ever so slowly, he lifted that plumed high hat off the ground, then half way, then all the way, up so that he was now nine feet tall in everyone's eyes. With what looked like the pointed hoof of the finest thoroughbred one has ever seen, he stepped out. The baton, raised as he simultaneously blew his signal for the band to follow, his stiff legs and pointed feet strutted across the field with the speed of triumph, the entire band right behind him. He didn't just march onto the field; he owned the field.

With that picture of our band competitor rushing, fleet-footed across the football field, I have walked through this life certain that the Army of God goose-steps that precisely and deliberately through this world. Why not? This is the Army that carries all of the strategies that win in the end. This is the Army that owns the field.

Also, as a result of the rushing Eddie and other moments even more directly connected with spiritual matters, I signed on to be in this Army, thinking perhaps I would be up close to the front--perhaps leading---when in reality, I am most often found back in the ranks. But---my point is---I signed up and I am there, armed and ready. I will strive to be what He wants me to be. Then one day striving will diminish, and my relationship with God will escalate higher into a life of faith and trust.

Once we move our own prancing feet to the side of the road and let Him do what He does, we move up through the ranks of the Army of God. In the year 2000, this truth came to me in the sound of a distant drumbeat from Kenya, Africa. Tammy had been working hard, but Tammy's earthly efforts were soon over. For me, Tammy's story showed the stages of moving up closer to God compressed into a very short few years. Also, I believe the African nurses saw that and were in awe of what they saw.

On the beat of that drum that sounds in the minds of the Kenyan people even when it isn't playing, the young women swayed and sang:

You've done enough, dear Sister,

You've done enough.

You've done enough, dear Sister,

You've done enough....

The Kenyan nurses-in-training at Kenwick Hospital in Kenya mournfully swayed, working their elegant hands to the music, eyes toward heaven, they repeated the phrase over and over again---You've done enough, dear Sister.

The countenance of the chorus of sorrow moved over us as we watched the recording of the African memorial for one of our own—Tammy King, obstetric nurse. More than once, Tammy had stood before our church congregation, telling us she was very much a homebody, loved her wonderful father and mother and could not believe that she, of all people, would be stepping out and actually going to Africa as a missionary. Would we join her in prayer and financial support as she began this venture? We had heard many similar stories, but this one especially had touched everyone because she was so admittedly green, sheltered and young. She became everyone's daughter and granddaughter at the moment of her poignant plea.

Now today we were assembled for her funeral. The news of the fatal accident came before the body arrived, but still we gathered for her funeral, needing to hear more of what had happened to our dear Tammy. She had built her faith quickly as missionaries often do. The three steps had been accelerated to prepare her for a quick and full life of service to God.

The report came back that Tammy, now in her late 20s, had driven a Land Rover from the Tenwick Hospital to Nairobi in order to pick up supplies and generally to have a few hours off from a demanding obstetrical nursing and teaching job at the hospital. The healthy foliage of the coffee bushes and other plants covered the hillsides and even crept close to the roadways on this sunny day in Africa. In a setting where the days and nights often blended into one very long shift at the hospital, having a few hours off was not common for Tammy. After all, babies were not born on cue or according to shift work. Because of her long work hours, this morning had developed into a lovely respite as she drove along in the all-wheel-drive vehicle widely used in these parts of Kenya.

Each mourner had a mental picture of Tammy's last hours. I could see Tammy driving her Land Rover, window down, arm resting on the window ledge, maneuvering the vehicle over the familiar, narrow bush-and tree-overgrown, rutted road.

Then the unthinkable happened.

As on her return trip, Tammy came near to the hospital area, a group of giggling children jumped out from the dense foliage along the road. There was no ditch or right-of-way space. When they leaped onto the road, they were into the line of traffic immediately.

Ever the champion for children, Tammy, avoiding the children, automatically steered her vehicle to leave the road and was soon swallowed by the density of the trees.

The children, possibly children belonging to her co-workers, halted in mid-run, looking on in horror as the familiar Land Rover had leaped over the slight build up of the grade, headed straight into a ravine, airborne, turning end over end over end like a lightweight toy. Finally it came to a solemn stop. Even now as we heard the retelling of the story, we held onto hope as long as the vehicle was catapulting its way over into the ravine. But now, the silence told the children, and told us, that the dream of becoming a nurse in a faraway land had come to a halt.

Soon Tammy's earthly body had turned cold, but the drumbeat and message of the song was warm and rocked the hearts of all who heard it—those in Kenya and those in her home church. And thus, her students, the nurses-in-training expressed their love and respect and taught all who could hear that in the deep soul-scraping sense of loss, a life is complete no matter if it ends at age 28 or 97, and that there comes a time, sometimes before death and certainly after death when one can sing—You've done enough, dear Sister. You've done enough.

Not unlike the deliverance in the Swing Low spiritual, Tammy had been delivered from the work-care of this world. Fortunately, for Tammy, her years of striving and faith building had been compressed into a shorter period than for many. Her payoff---she looked up and saw Jesus coming.

While Tammy's story illustrates the victory in death, our discussion moves on to show how we can and often do look up and see Jesus coming into our day-to-day lives, here and now.

Part 1

SWING LOW

SWING V-E-R-Y LOW, LORD

Marching along in the Army of God, trying my hardest to lower my fluffy, tall plumed hat to the ground behind me, but never accomplishing it, I began to note that human striving sometimes accomplishes very little. Then when I heard the nurses singing at Tammy's funeral, I realized that I was getting nothing accomplished, very quickly, with my own plans. Tammy had, but I hadn't.

At Tammy's funeral I had seen Jesus out in front of the singing nurses, the back-up singers, singing more loudly than they:

Judy, you've done enough, dear Sister,

You've done enough.

And then He added----JUDY,

LOOK WHAT YOU'VE DONE, CHILD!

See emphasis on that last part. In my funeral meditation, He and the singers sang that line at least twenty times, lest I would miss hearing it.

So WHAT HAD I DONE?

Well, there are the attempts to be extraordinary in an ordinary world. I soon realize that my desire to shine goes back to childhood when I sang for a nickel per song. That was followed by a competition in the fifth grade to outshine Janet and Billy on the learning curve. No victory there. Then I wanted more than anything to be the world's standard of youthful beauty. Movie Star picture collecting had brought that on. Doesn't every girl go through this phase? I longed to have the most beautiful wedding and the most perfect family. I would be the best teacher the Dept of Education had ever encountered. I longed to be the one in John Steinbeck's *The Moon is Down*, the one who rose from the ranks of ordinary folk and led the town folk out of crisis. In short, my picture of my statue in the ordinary world was to be extraordinary—probably not too different from that of most young people then and now.

The story of Gloria seems to fit right here; but sadly what I'm doing here is very typical of the striving one who has just been blessed, as at the funeral, and then quickly sees something in the day-to-day world that takes their attention from the blessing. See Ephesians 4:14 …forever changing our minds about what we believe….

Nonetheless, I read the following account in *The Indianapolis Star*. A summary goes like this:

Expectant mother Gloria, of Indianapolis gave birth to her baby girl, but the baby did not survive. However, today Gloria seems fine and is eating normally.

As I read this account, I studied the picture of Gloria who is now expected to have another baby as soon as she is well enough, depending on how she feels. Certainly she will be pregnant by the end of the year. Her suitor is Spike who is 21 years old. The pregnancy will last 16-17 months.

Oh, yes, I must tell you that Gloria is a white rhino.

Most would say Gloria might have already done enough with the nine pregnancies alone. And anyone reading the story feels a great sadness at the whole thought of the lost baby.

I look at her picture and doubt that Spike will be attracted to Gloria any time soon. Saying she is not pretty---extraordinary in an ordinary world—is selling the situation short. Gloria is said to be a white rhino, but Gloria isn't white. She isn't velvety black either. She's muddy looking, with incredibly scaly, dry skin, perhaps a low-thyroid condition. One has to wonder why God would allow Gloria to be called a white rhino when she isn't. This only emphasizes many other inconsistencies in her appearance. Upon researching the white rhino part, we learned that the "white" doesn't reflect the animal's color; it is derived from the Afrikaans's word for wide---referring to the wide mouths of the animals of that species.

And that brings me to another point---Gloria's mouth is too wide. But the wideness isn't as troubling as the convoluted configuration directly above it —an arrangement of nostrils, a tusk and eyes that are way too low on her face. Then to make matters worse, Gloria has been given a set of short, fat horns. Poor Gloria's neck is almost as wide as her shoulders, and she, even at age 30, already has the signs of aging, with a hump on her back. Her body looks as though it had started to be a hippopotamus, very low to the ground with the short stumpy legs that do not go with the rhino horns and tusks that show valor.

On top of all of this burden, Gloria has had a hard life, starting her child-bearing at age six or seven, and having babies every 2-3 years or sooner if the zoo officials have their way.

The white rhino is near extinction. But we humans look at the situation and say, "No wonder." God made the rhino to be less than ordinary in an extraordinary world. The symmetry of the face certainly is off. Beauty cream won't help.

We humans often have the same complaint. "God what were you thinking? I wanted to be extraordinary in an ordinary world, but right off, I didn't have much opportunity to be so."

Along with striving to be extraordinary in an ordinary world, I wanted to bring glory to God---and to do it with a flourish. I played the organ at our church when I was a teenager and led the singing even when I could hardly reach the middle notes, not to mention the high note. I was president of my youth group at church. I lived a moral life as a teen and was very proud of it. As an adult, I sponsored a girls' huddle in Fellowship of Christian Athletes, taught Sunday classes, and took the Bible study courses. When I wrote books, articles and poems, I wrote on only those subjects of eternal value. I wanted to bring glory to God.

Then one day Jesus said, "Be faithful to me where you are, in everything you do and THAT brings glory to me.

Along with being extraordinary and with bringing glory to God, I strategized to keep everyone that I knew in a healthy condition. I learned natural remedies, wise precautions and first response CPR. I kept lists of the best doctors in America, tracked their locations and specialties. I supported cancer research for children, homes away from home for ill children. I read about prescription drugs, even those I didn't need for me, or anyone I knew. I had wide and full file folders of clippings on every subject of health care. I stood guard, was vigilant in my studies of all disease.

Then Jesus said to me, "I gather my own into my arms, and I deliver them safely home." That's all he had to say on the subject.

To add to my striving to be extraordinary, to shine my light for God brightly, to keep everyone well, I kept the archives of the family, and memorabilia of a couple of towns---for good measure. Ah, journal keeping, the storing of memorabilia, photographs, clippings. Yes, God knows about the long history of journalizing in my family. I take full responsibility for this self-imposed, sometimes intrusive, laborious task of recording everything our family does, most things our small hometown and our present small community does. Following the example of my grandmother and my father whose journals started in 1935 and 1970 respectively, I keep a daily journal. Some days the entry looks like a diary; some days it looks like a journal. Having kept a journal for 39 years, I find no time to read what I have written. Because I wanted more from my father's entries, I have written full-page entries, a fact for which I may some day regret. One thing I have noted—the biggest, most stunning events in my life have received very little notice. After all, I was living to the full and had no time to record the thoughts of that day.

With my journalizing albatross around my neck, I one day heard Jesus say, "Lay not up for yourselves treasures on earth…" Why was I writing all of this? So I would be remembered, so this life could go on. It was as though I didn't want it to end and heaven to begin. Nothing in this world will last forever. It's all temporal—even my journals and file folders.

And what of the items I have preserved belonging to our parents, their memorabilia that meant so much to them—the estate jewelry, the cherry cupboard, the many quilts, the plaques and photos. Do I add these to my own more recent memorabilia? Does the next generation have to tote all of these items along with their own keepsakes?

Jesus rescues me from the heavy load: Lay not up for yourselves treasures that can turn yellow, that can burn, that can fall from a moving van, that can be stolen, that indeed are perishable....

The best way I can paint the picture of all of this striving is to recall the story of a special young woman in our lives—our niece, who volunteered for the Peace Corps in Senegal, Africa. When we asked her what kind of work she was doing there, she said, "I am involved in reforestation. In the Peace Corps lingo, we call it holding back the desert."

The mental picture that popped into my mind: a young girl with arms raised in protection of the great land of Senegal, literally holding back the unending winds that sweep over the Sahara pulling and scraping every living bit of vegetation in its path. The reality was that she was a part of a larger number of Peace Corps volunteers who were holding back the Sahara through reforestation and many other methods that would make the desert winds take notice.

But wasn't that image the image of what I was doing in my own life? The mighty desert was threatening to wipe out any evidence that I ever lived---so I was reforesting, replanting in an effort to hold back a force that is sweeping up everything in its path. This includes my mortality, my contributions.

So much for the rehash of what I have DONE and of what many of us have done on our own; now we look up to see Jesus coming to rescue all of us, from all of our striving and storing.

<u>Part 2</u>

TURNING

TURNING FROM OUR STRIVING

We turn from our striving. We make a conscious effort and pray to God to turn from our striving in whatever form it comes in. We do this only with God's strength to let go.

In a very small space we see how to turn from the striving.

The turn involves two steps:

1. We accept and hold onto the completed work that Jesus did at the Cross, when He took our sins away and paid the price for them.

2. We ask forgiveness for our sins that separated us from Him.

Part 3

FINDING

GRASPING THE HIGH FLYING BATON OF FAITH

After the turning, we reach for the Golden Ring and we find it in Luke 7:11-17 NIV

Soon afterward, Jesus went to a town called Nain, and his disciples, and a large crowd went along with Him.

As He approached the town gate, a dead person was being carried out---the only son of his mother, and she was a widow. And a large crowd from the town was with her.

When the Lord saw her, his heart went out to her and he said, "Don't cry."

Then He went up and touched the coffin, and those carrying it stood still.

He said, "Young man, I say to you, get up!"

And the dead man sat up and began to talk, and Jesus gave him back to his mother.

They were all filled with awe and praised God.

"A great Prophet has appeared among us, " they said. "He has come to help his people."

This news about Jesus spread throughout Judea and the surrounding country.

Finally, we are ready for deliverance. We say to Jesus, "Come Quickly."

SWING LOW, DEAR JESUS,

COMIN' FOR TO CARRY ME….

Soon I saw that I was not a vessel that God could use. The vessel that was me, was overflowing with attempts I had made---to do, to be.

Tammy King and the singing nurses learned it early on; long before the day she left the road to save the children. There must be an exchange. I must hand over the reigns and be saved from my own efforts. I truly must ask God to swing very low and deliver me from my own attempts.

Leviticus 16 tells us about the Scapegoat (a symbol for Jesus) taking our sins (often our strivings) on Him and carrying them out of town and into the wilderness never to be seen again.

Luke 7 shows us what happens when the widow has no more answers, no more efforts left and then looks up and sees Jesus coming into her circumstances. It was time to take Death in all of its forms to the edge of town and there pick up Life in exchange. Ephesians 4 says I must put off the old way and put on the new way, the way of Jesus.

So here I am in my marching clothes, making the turn. Not only have I never been able to own the field, as Eddie the drum major could do, I now know I must become as nothing so that God can put on Jesus Christ to transform me to something. Jesus saves, and it is an amazing thing to see.

The following are descriptions of times when Jesus appeared and faith took a step to higher ground:

<u>Story #1</u>

HE SPOKE THE WORDS THAT TURNED SOMEONE'S LIFE AROUND

Every parent and teacher has had times when a well chosen word would have been just the right word to turn their children (students) from their negative behavior. Most can count those "words in due season" on one hand. On the other hand, and many more hands, they can count the times when their words were most ineffective. The following are examples of simple answers to big problems. The few times when senior wisdom shines have to come from the heavenly realms. We mortals can't think fast enough to pull out such smart, pithy phrases that hit the matter with a powerful punch.

Punch #1—

The story of Josh Hamilton (*Beyond Belief,* Faith Works, 2008) made a great impression on me when I read how, after his drug use; his Granny helped him get back to the business of baseball. Josh had been the first player chosen in the 1999 baseball draft. Then in 2002, he began a downward spiral into illicit drug use, consequently began missing important appointments---like showing up for practice and games.

It was Grandma he went to; when every other person had decided he would not listen, no matter what they tried to do.

"Without Granny, I had no one. I saw the reality. I looked at the floor in shame. She said, 'Josh, you are such a good boy. There is so much good you could do with your life and instead, you're wasting it. I will not let it happen under my roof. If you're going to continue to do this, I'm kicking you out. It's your choice.'

She turned and walked away.

For some reason, my Grandma's words and the hurt in her voice and sorrow in her eyes, were embedded in my mind. I made a decision. I began to pray. There was a Bible in my room. I turned to James 4:7. "Humble yourself before God. Resist the devil and He will flee from you."

I repeated it and sweat, repeated it again. I talked out loud to the devil. At night I even dreamed I was hitting him with a baseball bat…"

Granny, with Jesus' help spoke the right words to turn Josh around.

Punch #2—

One of the leaders of our country was doing nothing with his life, living out his days on the beach. His guardians had tried everything to help him see how he was wasting the valuable life building years. They called his mother home to help influence him to change his ways. Leaving her overseas home, she came to spend several days with him before she addressed the problem at hand. Then she simply said, "Don't you think you're taking a pretty casual attitude about what you will do with the rest of your life." He says those words zeroed into his thinking and changed his direction then and there. He got on track to make something of himself.

No matter what political leaders we endorse, we do know that God works in governments, makes kings and deposes kings. Taking that knowledge into consideration, I see that He and his mother very likely collaborated on that statement.

Punch #3—

A carpenter from Kentucky was leaving his home to join the Army. His mother said to him, "I hate to see you go, but I know this is an opportunity for you. Just promise me one thing—that you will never do anything you will be ashamed of later."

He went through the years of service and didn't participate in any activity that he deemed he would be ashamed of the next morning. He never drank an alcoholic drink in all of that time while away in the Army. Today he marvels at the effect those few words from his mother had on his life.

Punch #4—

My own dad was having a glass of iced tea. He pulled out a cigarette and lit it. Then he became anxious. I could feel his fidgeting across the table. He turned to me and hurriedly said, "Judy, I have no right to say this, but please don't ever smoke a cigarette."

Then he suddenly began to choke up, and he quietly slipped out the kitchen screen door.

We never discussed that subject again.

I went on to college where girls sat in front of mirrors to practice holding their cigarettes in a sophisticated way. Smoking was the thing to do. Foolishly, I even served as critic on one occasion for what looked better to posing cigarette smokers. But I never smoked a cigarette. Ever. And for my genetic code, and me that decision probably was wise because my father's life was a short fifty-five years and his doctor had warned him the year of his death that smoking would shorten his life.

Into his remorse and sorrow for having set the example he didn't want me to follow; Jesus came.

Punch #5—

Becky was to stay at a friend's house in our small community. This girl was a church friend, so Becky's parents knew the family well. However, instead of going to this girl's house for the night, Becky went into town, about eight miles from us. She had been invited to the home of a popular high school friend. Living eight miles from town made Becky very far away from the town's activities. Her family's Sunday routine was set so, no chance that anyone in the family would see Becky at her friend's house.

However, her dad went into town on this Sunday night. This change in routine was unheard of. He drove in front of the girl's house. In front of the house was a carload of boys and girls laughing and talking and having a great time. Becky's dad drove his pickup beside the parked car and looking down into the parked car, exchanged glances with his daughter.

Then he drove away. This next morning they had a very quiet and miserable breakfast together. Not a word was said about the night before. Not then or ever.

Jesus had shown up into this humble man's routine. The father drove into town on nothing but " a hunch" (a good one at that) on this Sunday evening.

Punch #6—

Denzel allowed his boys to have a car. No rules about the general use of the car, just keep the car clean, and oh, yes, pay for the tires and gasoline.

Good deal!

Without further discussion, his boys, on their own, learned that no unsafe starts and slower driving made tires and gasoline last longer.

Jesus shows up when young drivers take the wheel of a car. He and Denzel worked together on this launching of two brothers into the driving world.

Punch #7—

A boy' s mother was at the hospital bed of her ill brother. While she was away, her son got into trouble and was taken to jail to spend the night. She returned home and couldn't find him. She called her husband who had taken his own shift at the hospital bedside. He suggested she call the county jail. Indeed their son, who had never been in trouble on this scale, was in jail.

The following morning the father and uncle went over to pick up the son when he was released from jail. On the way home, the boy finally said to his dad, "Go ahead and say it."

The father simply said, "I wouldn't have done to my mother what you did to yours for anything in this world."

The boy cried and cried and never went back to jail again.

Jesus and Father had perfect timing and chose words that touched on the relationship the boy treasured most—that with his mother.

Punch #8—

I was teaching a college class at a regional campus. Journals were submitted as part of the course work. I will never forget the journal entry of one young man. In fact, I included it in my book, *Picnic on the Grounds*, Ambassador Emerald Press, 2005. See the summarized account here:

"On this particular evening, I was returning pages from journal-keeping the students had submitted the week before. This journal was merely a recounting of the events of the week, making the writing more than a diary account, but rather a journal entry in which the student focused on one thought from the day and expounded upon it. A student, who was the same age as one of my own sons, submitted the entry that I will forever remember. The student, because of what he learned and what he taught me, is memorable indeed. He had an athletic, football player frame, dark hair and had a congenial manner. His interests ran along the lines of an outdoorsman —fisherman, hunter, and trapper. This journal entry for the previous Sunday read like this:

"Sunday—Today is a day of rest and to go to church. I don't rest and I don't go to church. The way I figure it, God's in my house as well as in church. I can be with Him at home. So on Sundays I stay home, take walks in the woods and commune with nature. Since I feel his presence there, I don't need the church."

At the next class meeting as I returned the journal pages, I watched to see his expression when he read my comment to this particular entry. Slowly, he turned the pages, almost every page had a comment on it, some in agreement, some humorous, but all related to what he had written on that page. Finally, he turned to the" Sunday entry" and began to read. Totally lost in what he was reading and totally unaware that he was being observed, he became quiet and thoughtful and remained so for much of the remainder of the class time.

Later, he told my son, "Your mother—she nailed me."

"Oh, really. What did she do?"

"Well, I had written an explanation of how I spend my Sundays—at home and not attending church. Then I explained that I could feel close to God while enjoying my down time as well as I could in church. And do you know what she wrote on my paper?

"No, but I think I might be able to guess the drift of what she wrote."

The boy laughed and said, "She wrote four words that I will never forget. Your mother wrote, "Where is the sacrifice?"

"Ya, she nailed me!

Well, more than a decade has passed since this incident, and I will always remember how I came to write those four words. Obviously, the object of this particular class was not to convince students regarding how they should spend their Sundays. Yet, I couldn't let this opportunity pass. The simplicity and direct phrasing were not my own. I heard the words as clearly as if someone were in the room and speaking them.

"Sacrifice? Where is the Sacrifice?"

The speaker to my mind? JESUS

Conclusion: Who puts these words in the thoughts and mouths of parents and teachers? I believe it is Jesus showing up at the time when a strong statement needs to be made.

Story #2

HE SHOWED WHAT COULD BE, VIA VICTORIA FALLS

In March 2010 fourteen-year-old Allison joined a youth mission going to Zimbabwe, Africa. Even though she was the youngest of the group of fifteen or so, the sponsors prudently guided all of the young people to teach classes at the camp, to interact with the young children, and to stay close to the program planned for them. On one occasion they left the camp and headed out to a close by animal park, but for the most part, they stayed together and in the camp. And that is as it should be, with a group of first-time, youth group missionaries. Nearby there are many deep gorges in which to fall. Sponsors take on a great responsibility leading the inexperienced on a mission.

However, by writing this, I wanted Ali to learn a principle that has served me well throughout the years. I wanted her to know how close she was to what some people have called the most magnificent sight on the globe. Their campground was approximately 15-20 miles from Victoria Falls. Victoria Falls was in the neighborhood! At the mission, she could have felt the spray from the tumbling waters! She was so close, yet because of the danger and the logistics of going to see the Falls, she couldn't go. Plus, because they couldn't go, the sponsors didn't let them know how close they were to this wonder of the world. Any sponsor knows there was wisdom in that.

But when we look at life in general, we see the analogy can be applied. It would shake us to the core if we knew that just around the corner, behind the next curtain, within calling distance; the most amazing thing exists for us to enjoy, to have as part of our life, to bless us.

I believe we need to live knowing this. Let's not quit quite so soon. David of the Bible ran from King Saul for thirteen years, but on the day starting the fourteenth year, the running stopped. David went on to become the greatest king Israel ever had, but better yet, he became "the man after God's own heart." By persevering, David didn't miss what was hidden yet still within his reach.

So what is so great about the Victoria Falls in your life? Well, the one in Allison's life is described like this: According to Google, the Victoria Falls is one of the greatest natural wonders of the world. They are a mile long curtain of falling water and are 355 ft high. The huge amount of spray from the falls shoots 1000 ft into the sky and can be seen 30 miles away. An African name for these falls: smoke that thunders. Always above these magnificent falls are rainbows. The best time to view them is during the rainy season of March to May (the dates when Ali and the youth group were there) when they are at their most impressive. The falls lay on the line between Zimbabwe and Zambia. The best head-on view of them is from Zimbabwe, but since 2006, most tourists view them from Zambia because of the political situation in Zimbabwe.

That was just one breath-taking opportunity with Ali's name on it. In a life there will be many, many Victoria Falls opportunities within a distance of only miles or minutes. Jesus doesn't need the restraints; sponsors do. He longs to show us Victoria Falls—and more wonders like this.

Story #3

HE MADE THINGS RIGHT WITH MRS. GEORGES' TEA SET AND MORE

After moving across the state, I was returning to teaching after a five-year break to be with our young children. When my contract was evaluated, the superintendent of schools said I lacked one teaching day of receiving the next $400 increment in pay. (Today, after having worked five years+ one semester, three of which were at the college level, I would estimate that$400 increment to be near $10,000+.) Our young family needed that money.

Plus it was really owed to me. Because of the challenging situation at this new position, I had been working in this new classroom for a day and half to prove I could handle this class. The man, who was leaving to form a privately owned theater in another state, taught a class made up of a few incorrigible students mixed with some other students who had had the misfortune of being placed in this class. For instance, one seventeen-year-old boy, the newspaper alleged, had earlier driven his friend and a fourteen-year-old girl four states away. Along the way, the fourteen-year-old girl had fallen from the pickup and was killed. Now the boy and his friend had returned home and were now back in school and in this class.

Could I teach the class? The answer came back that I could. Indeed I had taught these students ---making up that one day needed for the next increment. The superintendent couldn't see how that was so--no $400 increment for me.

As I drove the twelve miles home after that disappointing news of the lost increment, I was discouraged thinking of the injustice of it all. I parked the car and automatically walked over to the mailbox to take in the mail. Among the pieces I found a small note, definitely a lady's card…maybe it was an invitation or a cheery note. Nonetheless, I hurried to open it.

Mrs. Georges, a neighbor of my in-laws, wanted to give me a lovely silver tea set which she valued at---$400. That's right---$400. (Good measure – pressed down and running over.)

My $400 increment of pay came to me exactly 20 minutes after it had been taken away. As a young mother, I knew it would be decades before I would be able to own something so nice as a silver tea set. And both God and Mrs. Georges knew I liked lovely dishes and tea sets. She was giving it to repay my father and mother-in-law for taking her to doctor appointments, on little side trips and for daily checking on her welfare.

I will forever be amazed at two aspects of this gift.

1. The idea of giving me the tea set had to have been planted into Mrs. Georges' thoughts weeks earlier. Then she would have had the anguish of separation from her beloved silver. She would have had to gather her lovely notepaper to write describing her gift to me. She would have had to box it up and have it in the mail immediately after she sent this note. And—she didn't drive a car for any of this gathering of supplies. All of this passage of preparation had to include her prompt attention to drop the note in the mail at exactly one day before I would lose my $400 increment. Human maneuvering could not have accomplished this feat.

2. God had arranged for me to be compensated for the unjust loss with a gift custom-made to fit me. I didn't get the $400 in just any item, but it was an item that had my name written all over it. It was a shiny gift to play to my daydreams of lovely lady items that had been incubating since early childhood. When God does it, "it" always fits perfectly.

Another time when God made a situation right:

My family was suffering greatly. I called the bluff of the owner of the boutique I now managed and told her I needed shorter work days. Going in to work four days a week at 7:30 a.m. and leaving at 11:00 p.m., was not working for our family.

This was a hotel shop of choice items, and my friend and I decided I would like to work here. She was the buyer for this shop and six others like it. All of the items came from the West coast, therefore setting the collection apart from other shops in the area. Even though I was teaching college classes all of the hours I wasn't working in the shop, this little job was a fun thing to take on, and it followed a difficult time in our lives.

The sophisticated owner, a lady who did much of her own shopping in New York City's 5th Avenue shops, proceeded to pull out her compact mirror to powder her nose and slowly apply her lipstick as she answered my request. "In one month I will find your replacement. I'm sorry retail didn't work out for you." This methodical retouching of the lipstick incident constituted the one and only time I ever felt the sting of being terminated from a job. Not a good feeling, indeed.

I loved this shop. I had never had lovely accessorized suits and dresses. I knew I liked "pretty" too much, but this job came at a time when I needed "pretty."

After the termination, I went back into the shop and took my station as though nothing had changed in order to work out "my notice" of termination time. It was then that a very neatly dressed African American lady came into the shop to browse. I allowed her to enjoy the merchandise and then began to inquire, "What brings you into town?"

"The National Nazarene Convention. I am from Washington, D.C."

We had been advised that hundreds of delegates had come to this largest convention of the season. For all of us at the hotel, the mix of people, the other cities joining our city was the best part of our being there.

While she continued looking around the shop, I noted how graceful she was. It was as though she floated instead of walked. With her genteel manner and her manicured attire, she was set apart from the usual harried traveler who popped in to pick up something on her way elsewhere.

Finally, she worked her way up to the cash register, and with no information from me; she said she wanted me to have this card. "I sense that you are going through a difficult time."

The card read: Jesus is the only way.

Then she reached over and hugged me, pulling me to her beige suit where my own lipstick brushed a slight stain on her lapel. At that, I was most upset, but said nothing. No sooner had she come to the shop than she was gone. She hadn't purchased a thing. I looked for her over the next few days and never saw her again.

Where did she come from? Why did she come into the shop as if on cue after my forced retirement from the job? How did she know I was going through a rather difficult time?

Two things I learned from this incident:

1. A woman of God had appeared within moments of my receiving "the pink slip." The timing was too perfect, and she was too perfectly chosen for a mortal to have arranged it.

2. A woman of God will find service is messy. The hair will be rearranged; the suit will be smudged; the dog will bite the neighbor; the new chair will be scratched; the carpet will have a new spot on it, probably with red dye in it! Service is rarely neat as I saw all too clearly when I saw I had smudged the lapel of her once immaculate suit.

Story #4

HE SHOWED ME WHO I AM TO HIM

It only happened once, but once was enough. When Jesus speaks, the listener hears it well.

It was a Saturday morning after a rather difficult week. I awoke and lay in bed a few minutes to reflect on the activities of the past week and to review my plans for the day. The week had been filled with rejection and pointed to my loss of youth and opportunities to use my writing. I had come to the point in the road where it seemed I should give up my dream of making a huge difference in this world. Besides, I was obviously past the point of going out to market the result of my efforts, not looking young and energetic…or so I thought.

Then the most amazing thing happened.

As clearly as anyone in the room might have spoken to me, Jesus spoke directly to me. His voice came from within my mind, but I heard it as though he were in the room.

Very quietly and kindly, He said, "You want to know who I see when I look at you?"

"Yes. I do want to know."

"Well, get up and go into your office and look up at the picture on the highest shelf."

Which picture could that be? I had a number of pictures on that shelf. I jumped up and hurried to see what Jesus sees when He sees me.

There it was. The picture taken to announce my engagement to my husband was the best picture ever taken of me. I was 20 years old, had dancing eyes of hope and ambition. I was full of energy and youth.

"That's what you see when you see me?" I asked.

Quietly, and with finality in his voice, He said, "That's what I see."

Story # 5

HE DROVE ME TO SCHOOL AND TAUGHT MY CLASS

I had undiagnosed and therefore, untreated hypothyroidism. At the most unexpected times I would barely be able to think clearly would have blurred vision when I drove the car. In the year our second son had the brain tumor diagnosis, I was teaching in a city college. No doubt the combination of the stress of the newly discovered tumor and the hypothyroidism met head-on near the end of the semester.

One day near the time of the brain surgery, I started the 25-minute drive into the city to teach my morning class of English Comp. As I loaded my books in the car, I knew I was not well. It was as though some chemical was not reaching my brain. Light-headed and generally unnerved, I started driving. Half way to school, I realized I couldn't, shouldn't continue driving the car. Because I knew no one in this part of the city, I didn't really want to get out of the car. I began to pray. I asked Jesus to take over completely. I would trust Him. I knew this was a bold move on my part, but I had heard others say they had asked the same of our Savior, who is in the saving business here and now, and He had delivered. What else could I have done? A family member could have come to pick me up and have someone drive the car home, but then who would teach the class that was to start in less than one hour?

So off we went, Jesus steering through my hands at the wheel and me praying.

In fifteen more minutes, we did pull into the parking lot beside the building where my class was on the first floor, near the front side entrance of the building. Feeling just as uncertain as I had felt earlier, and being very much aware that I had not driven the car the last fifteen minutes of the commute, I knew I had to walk into the classroom and continue working with Jesus in this endeavor.

Not even opening the text I began to talk. I had an interesting question on current events that was a real attention-getter and opened a lively, interesting discussion in which everyone participated. Ah, full participation. This is good.

Then I gave a writing prompt that launched a volley of conversation followed by the best short writing assignment we had had all year. With these two successful portions of the two-hour class behind us, we then had a collaborative editing session in which everyone pulled out writings and participated.

The class ended. The time had flown by very quickly.

All of the time I taught the class I could not see the back of the room, and my balance was completely off. I cannot tell anyone more than I have written here about the time when Jesus taught my class. Wanting to write down that lesson plan from heaven, I could not. It wasn't mine.

I conclude that when we need Him most, when we've done our best on the other occasions, when we are treating Him with honor due Him, we can expect an experience that goes off the books for marvelous. He does come by. He does show up. You look up and there He is. (And, more often than not, the whole experience is solitary, given to you alone…..a prepared gospel for a prepared people.)

Story # 6

HE ACCOMPLISHED HIS WORK WITHOUT ME

With only one week's warning that my husband's twin brother was indeed very ill, we were listening for phone calls. But no one could have anticipated the one that came around noon on Saturday telling my husband his twin brother was now going to the Intensive Care Unit. At 5:00 p.m. his wife called saying he had only a 10% chance of survival. In an hour we were on our way to the airport to fly to be with him.

While we were flying near Atlanta, getting ready for touchdown there to change planes, I became restless, noted that my husband had stopped reading and was deep in his thoughts. I prayed to God asking Him to make it possible for us to get to the bedside of my husband's brother before his passing. We wanted him to know we would see him again and pray together for that reunion. No sooner than I ended that prayer, I picked up my book by Henry and Mel Blackaby, What's So Spiritual About Your Gifts?, and read what I now paraphrase---God gets his work done. If I am not in the spot to do the work, God gets someone else to carry His message, to do His work.

When I read this, I knew I had heard the answer to my prayer. I suspected that there had been a change at the hospital. God was preparing me and telling me---Eternity doesn't depend on certain mortals speaking My words. Rest assured--I will get My work done.

We changed planes in Atlanta. Walking down the long corridor to our plane, we suddenly heard someone yelling, "Uncle Barry. Uncle Barry." It was my husband's niece, and Larry's daughter, flying in from New York City. Lots of hugs and tears and then she said, "Chris called and Dad passed on about ten minutes ago." We were really jolted by this news. All three of us were crying, and it was time to board our plane. The clerk at the desk looked at us and quickly said, "I'll find an area where all of you can sit together." And she did.

We reached the hospital over two hours after Larry had died. The staff, aware that his daughter and twin brother were flying to reach the hospital, made it possible for us to go to the room to sit beside his body.

God can do anything. He can even make the dead convey his message to us. Larry had laugh crinkles at the corners of his eyes, and his mouth was turned in a soft smile---the look one has when he sees an acquaintance after a long absence. I believe God wanted me to see this and to point it out to my grieving husband.

It was well with his soul. Seeing his parents would have been welcomed. But this was more than that---It was truly well with his soul.

Perhaps a nurse or a hospital worker had taken her job just for times like this. God had been with Larry in his passing.

Each of us had our own view of this final visit with our loved one. For me, it became even more than a goodbye. It had become a revelation of what I had just read in the Blackaby book. God wanted me to see that He had been there in Larry's passing. And He wanted me to see that He had been there in order that I could pass what I had seen onto his twin brother.

Story #7

HE USED HARRY EMERSON FOSDICK TO CONSOLE ME

It was one of those times that Charles Dickens referred to when he wrote in *A Tale of Two Cities*, "It was the best of times and the worst of times." We were heading to New York City for the graduation from Columbia University of our niece. It had been ten months since her father had died and six weeks since her brother Chris had died of Hodgkins Disease. We wanted to help her celebrate this event and try to momentarily suppress our compounded sorrow.

Words had been carefully chosen. We focused on seeing the sights of New York that had meant something special to her. We walked in Central Park. She took us on a bus tour of Lower Manhattan. We greeted her high school friend who had come over to Battery Park from his home on Staten Island. We had brunch in a sidewalk café, and now it was time to head to Riverside Church at the corner of the Columbia Campus. Today, with actress Ruby Dee as one of the speakers; Libby received her Masters' Degree from the prestigious Teacher's College. We were very proud of her for persevering through the hard times, not the least of them the serious illnesses and deaths of both her father and brother.

As time came for graduation, Libby had gone on to join her classmates. Her mother, her aunt, Barry and I stood on the sidewalk slowly approaching the door to Riverside church that looked, in all its beauty, more like an architectural wonder. As the day went by, conversation had not become easier. We were still trying not to allude to the very big item in our lives. So we muddled through and finally made our way past the organizers at the door and found ourselves in the vestibule of this wonderful, old church. I looked at the ceilings, the archways, the naves, the many little areas bathed in fresco and wonderful murals. Since teaching was my own area of concentration, this campus, this Teacher's College was often alluded to in my teaching communiqués. If it had been another time, this day would have been spent differently as a light-hearted adventure for all, but we could not shake the sadness that lurked very close to all of us. Finally, I decided I would concentrate on taking away every good thing from this day. I would really look for solace and something uplifting.

It was then that I looked up above a registry and saw a portrait with the name inscribed on brass below—Harry Emerson Fosdick. I know him. Now how do I know this name? Had I heard it while I was teaching, or was it in church, or was it in historical reading? I didn't have the answer. We made our way through the many halls and finally to our assigned seats in the auditorium. Looking around the enormous room at the stained glass, the guest speakers, I continued to run Harry Emerson Fosdick through my mind.

It was about the time that Actress Ruby Dee stood to speak that I remembered where I had heard the name Harry Emerson Fosdick. My sister Karen had been in the high school choir, and they had sung, "God of Grace and God of Glory," written by Fosdick. The words to that wonderful song of the church had blessed me then, and they were indeed blessing me now. Having my own little moment there in the pew, I slowly pulled out the phrases of that song and marveled that into that educational and exceedingly tolerant setting, Jesus came. He came and silently sang the words with me.

I also marveled that he had chosen Harry Emerson Fosdick, because in the following weeks after I read Fosdick's book, *The Living of These Days*, I realized his interpretation of Christian's journey in this world and my own differed. But God knew my only association with Fosdick on this graduation day was with this great hymn and that's all He wanted me to focus on. The words to that hymn bring Jesus right there to minister and comfort.

GOD OF GRACE AND GOD OF GLORY

God of grace and God of glory,

On Thy people pour Thy power.

Crown Thine ancient church's story,

Bring her bud to glorious flower.
Grant us wisdom, grant us courage,
For the facing of this hour,
For the facing of this hour.

Lo! The hosts of evil 'round us,
Scorn Thy Christ, assail His ways.
From the fears that long have bound us,
Free our hearts to faith and praise.
Grant us wisdom, grant us courage,
For the living of these days,
For the living of these days.

Cure Thy children's warring madness,
Bend our pride to Thy control.
Shame our wanton selfish gladness,
Rich in things, and poor in soul.
Grant us wisdom, grant us courage,
Lest we miss Thy kingdom's goal,
Lest we miss Thy kingdom's goal.

Set our feet on lofty places,
Gird our lives that they may be,
Armored with all Christ-like graces,
In the fight to set men free.
Grant us wisdom, grant us courage,
That we fail not man nor Thee,
That we fail not man nor Thee.

Save us from weak resignation,

To the evils we deplore.

Let the search for Thy salvation,

Be our glory evermore.

Grant us wisdom, grant us courage,

Serving Thee Whom we adore,

Serving Thee Whom we adore.

Lyrics by Henry Emerson Fosdick, 1930

Music by John Hughes, Cwm Rhondda, 1907

Lyrics based upon Joshua 1:9

"Be not afraid…for the Lord thy God is with thee."

Story # 8

HE ANSWERED PRAYERS PRAYED BY THE MOTHER SEVEN YEARS BEFORE HER DEATH

When my husband and his twin brother left home to go to college, it had been only two years since their older brother Lee had died of spinal meningitis after a four-day illness. Naturally, this mother of twin sons felt a heavy burden to pray for their safety, for their choices and for their success. She prayed for her sons through it all. Because I was also on campus, my future husband spent lots of time with me. That left his twin brother to find other companions. These friends offered both good and not so good companionship. Through it all she prayed. And she prayed when her sons were married. She prayed when their children were born. She prayed when they took their jobs, moved their families. She prayed for things she knew about and prayed for things she didn't know about. Then she died seven years before the day of one of her sons' own passing.

It was in the hospital room beside his now cold body that I realized—a mother's prayers are being answered today, and she has been gone from us seven years now.

Jesus can show up and do anything. Just because someone has died, that doesn't mean their prayers died with them. No prayer goes unanswered. No prayer is wasted, lost in the slush pile. Each prayer is an audience with the Divine, and the Divine Savior can pull what some might call dead back to life.

Story # 9

HE TOOK ME THROUGH THE WEEKEND OF SHOCK TIMES THREE

The last days of October and the first couple of days of November 1978 will forever be remembered by me. Three fourteen-year- old boys tell the story. First, there was the boy who was in my class at school. He had leukemia. In late August when he enrolled in my honors English class, I was briefed about his disease and the plans to take him to Fred Hutchinson Cancer Research Center in Seattle soon after school began. The shuffle of his feet, the sprigs of the hair coming back in, the many adjustments he had to make to his schedule told me that his body was putting up its best fight, a fight he might not win. To help this class of 30 students understand what he was going through, I did much research on leukemia and knew just about all a layperson could know about the ever changing treatment for this vicious disease, particularly vicious in the last days of the 1970s. The boy went to Hutchinson and our class sent him handmade posters, which the family held up outside the plastic bubble he lived in around the clock. His immunity had been reduced to near zero as he endured his treatment. Two months into the school year, he died there in Hutchinson.

Two weeks later our fourteen- year- old son was with his friend on fall break from school. They were working on a joint project for history class. They would build a model of the battle at Jamestown, Virginia. But first they would go to Jamestown and see what really transpired there. As the four days wound down, Steve's stamina dropped to near zero, his complexion turned to ghostly white, and his neck was swollen from the earlobes down to the collarbone. He and the host family returned home while he was still strong enough to cover his illness, but we could see he must have a serious case of strep throat with all of that swelling, and tomorrow he was to return to school. The trip to the local hospital revealed more than we could have ever imagined. The intern on weekend duty suspected he should go to Riley Hospital For Children immediately for it looked like he might have leukemia. Our son went and he did have the disease I had been researching for the past two months.

Meanwhile, on the weekend of our son's diagnosis, a group of boys from the high school where I taught English went on a hayride. I was the sponsor to this counterpart girls' group of athletes; I knew the young men and the sponsor well. Often we combined the two groups, but since my son was in the hospital, the girls had not been included on this hayride.

While on this light-hearted adventure, a fourteen-year-old boy who had little experience with farm equipment decided to jump from the moving wagon to the moving tractor so he could ask the sponsor and owner of the tractor a question. This boy was the only fourteen-year-old on the wagon. The other boys were the more experienced in sports and were the upperclassmen. Being the only freshman on board, he decided to jump up on the tractor and talk to the sponsor as they drove over the backfields of the sponsor's childhood farm.

The fourteen-year-old made the leap, but didn't connect with the bar on the back of the tractor. Consequently, he fell to his death under the weight of the huge tractor's wheels. The wife of the sponsor herded the other boys and instructed them to go directly home. She ran over the fields to the house to call for help. On that lone hillside, no doubt, Jesus appeared. For there is no way a sponsor could take in the enormity of such an accident.

On Monday morning all of the news hit hard---our son had leukemia. Also the fourteen-year-old had fallen to his death from the wagon. The death of the fourteen-year old student of mine, occurring out of state, was still fresh in all our minds.

I was thirty-five and most of the people involved were quite young. How did we endure that weekend? Jesus appeared. The big things did not change. Two boys had leukemia, one had died from it, and one boy had fallen to his death from a hayride. Those things remained, but hundreds of the smaller miracles unfolded. People became messengers of God. Suddenly the ones involved saw the smaller miracles. Such little things, they were, yet so big. Volunteers stepped up to help the families of all the young people involved. In all of the planning and hospital visits, what might have taken three hours was completed in minutes. Parking places materialized out of nowhere. And the wonderful presence of Jesus our Savior stayed near all day and all night for weeks and weeks and weeks.(Hebrews 13:5 and 8)

Story # 10

HE ANSWERED AN INDIANAPOLIS PRAYER IN FORT LAUDERDALE

I wrote the following in my book, *A Whirlwind's Breath,* originally published by Guild Press in 1998, and republished by Author's Tranquility Press in 2024:

Only five months after the surgery to shunt the pressing brain tumor, our son Brian wanted to go with his friends to Florida over Spring Break. Even though he was going to Fort Lauderdale, reportedly a spring break place where few people eat right, get plenty of sleep; we reasoned that he was becoming dangerously dependent on being close to his doctors, to us. This trip would break that cycle of fear. Plus, the friend who had been with him through it all, knew the dangers, knew how he needed to get away from the claustrophobic life sheltered near his doctors. And so, we endorsed the trip for this 20-year old.

"Three nights into the trip, our phone rang at 11:00 p.m. Brian was calling from the emergency room of a hospital in Ft. Lauderdale.

"Oh!" was my standard reply to such unexpected phone calls. Then after that unusual response, I blurted out, "Brian, are you all right? What has happened?"

By now Barry was on the extension phone as Brian began to tell us about the numbness all down his left side. I diagnosed as he spoke. "He's having a stroke" was the repeated recording in my brain.

Trying not to sound alarmed, we gave the insurance numbers so the non-English speaking hospital staff could examine him. Our final words were, "Call when you return to your motel room. We will not go to sleep until we hear from you."

Thinking ahead even as we said our goodbyes, I was mentally making airplane reservations, when I remembered that a major airline was on strike. Few could obtain a ticket to Ft, Lauderdale over spring break even in the best of times.

As I thumbed through the phone book, I half-heartedly prayed. The only audible part of that prayer was a one-liner, "Lord, send him a companion, a friend who knows the way." (His friends from home had gone on to Key West for a couple of days while he said he just needed to hang around there and rest.) Then as I frantically continued to make a plane reservation, I thought to myself, 'What a dumb prayer!' My son is having a stroke, and I am praying that he have a companion, a friend!"

Telling myself he was surely becoming paralyzed on the left side, I ripped open the telephone book and called every airline company listed on the page. (His surgery the previous November had been emergency surgery to prevent paralysis. Therefore, paralysis was a real possibility, I reasoned). Finally, I relayed our problem to an agent who earnestly began to search for a spare ticket to Ft. Lauderdale. In a few minutes she had located a one-way ticket out of Cincinnati, leaving the following morning at 7:30 a.m.

Barry and I discussed the plan for him to drive to Cincinnati, take the one-way ticket to Ft. Lauderdale, and then rent a car to bring Brian home. Our plans were set by the time the phone rang again around 1:00 a.m. With me hovering near the phone, Barry took the call.

Immediately, I could detect a new tone in their conversation. They were discussing the problems of communication with people who do not speak English. What kind of a conversation was this? Here he was having a stroke, and they were discussing culture shock!

Very soon Brian told his dad he didn't want anyone to fly down. He said he felt very tired and simply needed a good night's rest to let the medication do the work. Then he said, "I need to talk to Mom."

Certain I could persuade him to come home, I took the phone. I could hardly believe the change in his voice from the earlier conversation.

"Mom, you know how you and I have talked about coincidences that happen, weird stuff—you will not believe what happened to me tonight. I was leaving the hospital with my medication, feeling more upset, more tired and sicker than I have ever felt. Everyone around me was Spanish-speaking, and my friends, not knowing how sick I was, were spending the night in Key West. I felt very much alone. Almost everyone here in the waiting room tonight had overdosed on something; most emergency room patients were filthy. What a depressing place!

I called a taxi and waited. By the time I had stepped into the cab, I was ready to break down. I never felt so alone. When the cab driver turned to ask me where I was going, I could not believe that yet another person spoke in Spanish. I guess I must have looked as bad as I felt because without hesitation, the cab driver turned back around and picked up a card from the front seat, then reached back to give me that card. In my weary state, I do not even know why I looked down at it. I guess I wanted to see what Spanish looks like. You will not believe what that card said in English.

Let not your heart be troubled;

Ye believe in God,

Believe also in me.

In my Father's house

Are many mansions:

If it were not so,

I would have told you.

And if I go and prepare a place

For you, I will come again,

And receive you unto myself;

That where I am, there ye may be also.

John 14: 1-3 in the KJV

"Mom, I know you have said things like that have happened to you, but that was too-o-o-o weird. Where did that taxi driver come from? I do know he was in the right place at the right time. Well, I am exhausted. I know I will feel better tomorrow."

Ecstatic, I put the receiver down. I recalled my mumbled, one-line prayer, "Lord, please send him a companion, a friend who knows the way." (Or was it THE WAY?) I had prayed, but had not really expected to receive an answer. Certainly I had no idea that God, who was hearing my prayer as it floated through the heavens above Indianapolis, could act on the object of that prayer in Ft. Lauderdale.

The results of prayer exceed what we mortals could have done. It was far better that I pray in Indiana than that I sit in the hospital waiting room in Ft. Lauderdale. My presence and care would be minimal compared to what God could do with a prayer from Indiana or anywhere.

As I put down the receiver of the phone that night, I remembered a discussion I had heard that had undoubtedly influenced my conclusions on this late night vigil.

A few months earlier, we were seated at a church carry-in dinner. Several women were talking about how they worry when their sons and daughters are out at night. Fortunately for us, Tom joined the group. When he could no longer tolerate what he was hearing, he calmly, but firmly said, "It constantly amazes me that you mothers believe you can protect your child better than God can."

And so, Jesus and Tom with Him, showed up on that occasion and many, many more like it.

Story # 11

HE SHOWED ME THE PATH TO THE TOP

Years of studying the world's literature led me to looking into the world's religions, for literature of a group of people is inevitably intertwined with the religion of that group. Indirectly, through characterization in the classics or directly, through reading some of the papers of the world's religious leaders, I found there are many admirable qualities in the practices of each of the major religions. Most promote ethical teachings and teachings for human interaction and fairness that stand as great manuals for living. And— in some cases, these appear to come near to matching or even sounding like those of Christianity.

For instance, teachings on how to handle material accumulation, the storing of treasures, the pure and simple appreciation of the natural world… all of these and more serve as valid guides to living. All considered, one could say, "It appears that almost all religions have teachings that complement each other." As I look at this conclusion, I see why young people or searching people blend all religions into one and do not see one religion as exclusive.

Then into our investigations comes the popular maxim to show tolerance in our communities and certainly when interacting with others regarding religious differences.

In regard to tolerance, I believe Scripture says it best, "If possible, as far as it depends on you, live at peace with everyone." Romans 12:18 NIV

"Strive to live in peace with everybody and pursue that consecration and holiness without which no one will see the Lord." Hebrews 12:14 NIV

When it comes to matters of eternal salvation there comes a necessary huge divide. Tolerance no longer can apply when we look to see how a given religion includes Jesus into its teachings and it does not. Then assessment always comes back: Only Christianity says Jesus is the Son of God and Savior of the World.

I remember the story attributed to the Tony Evans family of the Oak Cliff Bible Fellowship Church in Dallas. Dr. Evans was telling about his son's mountain climbing on one of the highest peaks in the world. The son told his father that there are many trails up the mountain. They are good trails as far as they go, but eventually all of these trails, except one, will come to a dead end. In order to reach the summit, the climber must find that one trail that goes all the way to the top.

The minister went on to explain that is the way it is with the world's religions. All of them have wonderful principles for living a life of service, for living an ethical life. You name them: Judaism, Islam, Hinduism, Buddhism, Christianity, and many more. But there is only one that will take you all the way to the Throne of God. The other trails stop just short of taking you on in. Jesus said, "I am the way." And the only religious group whose members believe that Jesus is Son of God and that He is the only way to the Father God is Christianity. All of the others take you up higher and higher, but eventually all of them fall short of taking you all the way to the summit.

And it is on the summit that we turn and face the world and shout, "Victory."

For me, the true test came when I went through two life and death situations with those who practice religions other than the Christianity I practice. In both cases, as the severity of the situation escalated, the view of the dead end trail came into view. Those who were so hopeful and passionate in their view of life as they practiced their other religions began to look at death as something they should respect, give a moment of silence to, and then move on in a cyclical way to helping the next ailing person in the same situation, and the next and the next. They reached a dead end when they saw a big NOTHING up ahead.

Jesus offers Eternal Life at that point. For the Christian, death is nothing more than passing through a veil into a wonderful forever. My respected friends and I could no longer communicate, for we saw two different futures.

Jesus said, "I am the way." At the juncture of life and death, a person sees that very clearly. Jesus appears and carries the one dependent upon Him on to the summit.

Story # 12

HE AWAKENED ME WITH THE CLIP CLOP OF A HORSE AND THE SWISH OF A PASSING BUGGY

Leap Year 2008

Mother died just hours before February 29. For some reason, the date was a slight comfort. We did not want to guess at the date each year, to have that imaginary anniversary of her passing. Her father had died during a Leap Year, and the whole Leap Year-thing was becoming a habit we wished would end soon.

I drove her Oldsmobile to her house in Orleans on the corner of 6th and Jackson. This was where I wanted to spend the next couple or three weeks. Being in this house all alone at night would give me an understanding of many unknowns. All day my sister, brother-in-law and I sorted and worked. Then at night, by my own choice, I stayed in Mother's house, meditated on what we had just seen unfold.

And so it went, night after long, busy day of sorting, after night, after night, after night I stayed in the bedroom with my head resting only a few feet from the side road, listening for answers to the questions people have been asking since time began.

It is significant that only the mailbox and a little patch of grass lay between 6th Street, and me for each morning I awoke to the trot of horses pulling an Amish buggy on that street. In this world there is little to compare with the peaceful rhythmic trot of horses making their way across country to a morning appointment. This clip-clop will forever be associated with any shred of my understanding of Mother's life and death. In the months to come, long after I had returned to my own home, I heard this rhythmic cadence of clip clop over and over again as I asked the questions, remembered, asked more questions and received just enough insight to help me emerge from what had been one of the traumatic times of my life.

It may have been the final application of understanding—I don't know—but a few months after Mother's death, I came upon a cassette tape that had been handed to my mother in an attempt to comfort her in her last days. Not being one to work with machines, she had kept it in its place and never listened to it.

Now I was discarding odds and ends as one keeps beside a sick bed, when I decided these months later to sit down and listen to this tape. Somewhere between "I Come To The Garden Alone" and the picture of the approaching Jesus, I did not hear the answer to my questions, I received something better and much more satisfying.

The whole revelation rested in the story found in Luke 7:11-17. As my thoughts magnified what I had heard on the tape, I mixed the widow's story with our story and the cadence of the whole collaboration was that of the horses' hooves:

I saw a widow dressed in black, walking behind a simple wooden casket. Closest friends carry this homemade box. A procession of citizenry follows. First the son's body on the way to the burial, then those who carry him, then the widow followed by the people of the small town of Nain. From the first to the last, no one really knows the answers to the questions of sickness and death. Obediently they move along, doing the duty that respect demands.

Clip Clop Clip Clop Clip Clop Clip Clop Clip Clop Clip Clop

Death is simple. It has roots in the animal world. One comes to the end of the trail and can go no farther. The journey ends.

Death is a community endeavor. It involves making the yeast rolls for the funeral meal. The whole community participates in carrying the body to the grave.

It's a remembering thing— death is about bringing up pictures that were filed away. It's a final chapter. It brings to mind that all things good, enjoyable, precious, lovely, deep purple, bright orange, lush will fade and die from this present form.

Clip Clop Clip Clop Clip Clop Clip Clop Clip Clop Clip Clop

Death involves---

"It's a fatal disease. We can make you comfortable."

Life here is grand

With friends I love so dear,

Comfort I get from God's own Word

Yet when I face the chilling hand of death…Where could I go? Where could I go? Where could I go?*

Clip Clop Clip Clop Clip Clop Clip Clop Clip Clop Clip Clop

The procession isn't slow because the body is heavy. Rather the procession is slow because each townsperson must have time to reflect on the meaning of leaving town with the body in tow.

*From the hymn "Where Could I Go But To The Lord?"

What does this mean---we're going to bury Jake?

And the widow corrects, "We're going to bury Jakey.

Clip Clop Clip Clop Clip Clop Clip Clop Clip Clop Clip Clop

First they take Jackson Street across First Street; then they come to Second. On Second, they see flashes of every loss they ever had. The broken vase, the lost wage, the lost promise, the lost crop, the lost hired hand, the lost joy, the lost youth, the lost loved one. All of the losses seem to come out of the dust of the street. All make sure they are acknowledged before they evaporate.

Clip Clop Clip Clop Clip Clop Clip Clop Clip Clop Clip Clop Clip Clop

Crossing Second and moving onto Third Street, the procession stalls to allow the cross traffic to move through---In the halt, the mourners see their own loved ones, the aunts, the uncles, grandparents, cousins all the throng that have gone on before them. They see the personification of love, shock, longing, and fear, all of the above in every configuration as they move toward Fourth Street.

Clip Clop Clip Clop Clip Clop Clip Clop Clip Clop Clip Clop Clip Clop

It is in the intersection of Jackson and Fourth Street that the waves of anger move in like a squall in the weather. The procession halts once again. This time the people balk at the necessity to bury this loved one. Why has this happened to Jake? And the widow corrects them, "Jakey." Then in their stew, they stumble, they growl, some curse the day and the hour, they mumble, they vow that they will see this through, but never again will they be duped. Enough of the trick playing; Enough of this eating the green leafy and then falling over dead.

Clip Clop Clip Clop Clip Clop Clip Clop Clip Clop Clip Clop Clip Clop

The procession now reaches Fifth Street; Only one more block to go. The anger dissolves into a mush of pitiful sobbing. The procession formation begins to blur, and the body of the deceased is no longer right ahead of the mourners. It's not even moving. Then it lists sideways. Then it has lost its way.

Death is death. This isn't a band performance. This is death. Limestone Carving Final.

Clip Clop Clip Clop Clip Clop Clip Clop Clip Clop Clip Clop Clip Clop

"O, Soul, are you weary and troubled?"

Clip Clop Clip Clop Clip Clop Clip Clop Clip Clop Clip Clop Clip Clop

And the story goes that the widow and the procession moved through Jackson and 6th and making their last approach to the cemetery, they buckled at what they saw up ahead. It wasn't an apparition, a ghost of Jake, a comet, a gigantic amethyst jewel fallen from the wall of heaven…

It was JESUS.

He had heard of the funeral over in Nain, and he had come quickly and brought an entourage with him. He had heard of the loss, the disappointment, the sorrow, the fear for provision for this lone widow, the whole town had been calling out and JESUS had heard. He was coming around the bend in the dusty road.

No mistaking where He was headed, for he was moving quickly toward the cemetery gate, toward the pine box, toward the hurt, the pain…like a laser beam He was headed toward the exact point of misery. And He knew exactly what to do. He held out life-filled hands. He rested them on the loss, the hurt, and the dead body. JESUS heard and he came and said, "Don't cry." And then He moved closer and said, "Young man, I say to you, get up!"

Did you hear that?

He said, "Don't cry." And then He said, "Young man, I say to you, get up."

Clip Clop Clip Clop Clip Clop Clip Clop Clip Clop Clip Clop Clip Clop

The dead man sat up and began to talk, and JESUS gave him back to his mother.

That was huge, but somehow the people in the procession could see clearly.

Somehow in their weariness, they could understand that they had received only a sampling

And the procession sang out …

"The half cannot be fancied…

Oh, there He'll be still sweeter

Than He ever was before." *

*From the hymn

"Still Sweeter Every Day"

Some continued:

"Thou the spring of all my comfort,

More than life to me

Whom on earth have I beside Thee?

Pass me not, O Gentle Savior."*

The story continues as they stood there in the cemetery among the dogwood and limestone, they were filled with awe and praised God. A great prophet has appeared among us," they said. "God has come to help His people."

The news about JESUS spread throughout Judea and the surrounding country. One of the first people told about this history-making day was John the Baptist, the cousin, and all of those with him. That announcement must have gone something like a chorus with hymn writer Thoro Harris:

Who can cheer the heart like Jesus,

By His Presence all divine?

True and tender, true and precious,

O how blest to call Him mine!

All that thrills my soul is Jesus,

He is more than life to me;

And the fairest of ten thousand

In my blessed Lord I see. **

Clip Clop Clip Clop Clip Clop Clip Clop Clip Clop Clip Clop Clip Clop

*From the hymn

"Pass Me Not, O Gentle Savior"

**From the hymn,

"All That Thrills My Soul Is Jesus"

Story # 13

BEST OF ALL, HE LED ME TO THE MESSAGE OF LUKE 7: 11-17
NIV

Luke 7:11-17

11. Soon afterward, Jesus went to a town called Nain, and his disciples and a large crowd went along with him.

12. As he approached the town gate, a dead person was being carried out—the only son of his mother, and she was a widow. And a large crowd from the town was with her.

13. When the Lord saw her, his heart went out to her and he said, "Don't cry."

14. Then he went up and touched the coffin, and those carrying it stood still. He said, "Young man, I say to you, get up!"

15. The dead man sat up and began to talk, and Jesus gave him back to his mother.

16. They were all filled with awe and praised God. "A great prophet has appeared among us," they said. "God has come to help his people."

17. This news about Jesus spread throughout Judea and the surrounding country.

The question: Was that part of you or me in that procession leaving town? I believe I have been in that procession carrying the dead parts of me that needed to be rejuvenated by the healing touch of Jesus. While the widow of Nain carried the ultimate death, we carry the little-foxes-that-spoil-the-vines in our parcels. Here was a woman who needed the chariot to come and swing low for her on this day of the death of her only son. That chariot came.

While there were many marvelous happenings in the life and ministry of Jesus, this one about the raising from the dead of the widow's son was carefully singled out for us to read. It speaks to us.

Once we allow Jesus to deliver us, to carry away our dead or to revive it again, we find deliverance in forms we never expected. Our deliverance comes in life and in death, at early stages and in later years; it may be relayed to us through a friend or one who is not normally so friendly; it may come directly or indirectly straight from the hand of God. Yes, God, the Creator, is never limited in how He delivers his aid.

One day I thought I would have some fun with composing a picture of the appearance of the approaching Jesus---according to what I had been told. This is what I put together:

RECIPE FOR THE ESSENCE OF THE APPROACHING JESUS

Pour the following (in equal parts) into the blender. Press BLEND. The resulting blend will be my picture of what the approaching Jesus must look like:

1 cup of chariots of fire running in a circle

1 cup of very soft whispers

1 cup of a lion and a lamb napping side by side

1 cup of eyes looking back at you after the denial

1 cup of a patch of choice land

1 cup of a coat of many colors

1 cup of the final stone in the wall of protection

1 cup of a cruise in the latched down ark of safety

I cup of the entrance into the city amid waving palms

1 cup of a razor-sharp split in the waters you must cross

1 cup of dew on the roses

1 cup of the breath of the Holy Spirit settling over all

1 cup of a few hours of blindness while on the road

1 cup of a sterling cup in a sack of grain

1 cup of six colors morphing into the canopy of the heavens

1 cup of the white horse with a white-clad rider

1 cup of ten laws to make sure you have boundaries

1 cup of a bridegroom approaching a bride in waiting

1 cup of a pig farmer running to meet his son

1 cup of a strolling companion who joins you on the road

1 cup of alpha and omega rushed together

Other Books by Judy Chatham:

———————

Picnic On The Grounds (the striving), Ambassador International, 2005

A Whirlwind's Breath (the turning in the trial),
Author's Tranquility Press, 2024

The Amber Necklace (the victory), Author's Tranquility Press, 2024

A Journal For Girls, Author's Tranquility Press, 2024

Books co-written by Judy:

Windows of Assurance with Billie Cash, available at
www.billiecash.com.

The Bridge with Betty Rich Hendon, available through
www.bettyhendon.com.

Judy also collaborated with Dr. George Rawls, then with the Indiana University School of Medicine, on his book, *Papa I Want To Be A Surgeon*

For copies of earlier books, contact Judy through her website
www.judychathambooks.com or through:

Judy Chatham / Author's Tranquility Press
3900 N Commerce Dr. Suite 300 #1255
Atlanta, GA 30344
www.authorstranquilitypress.com
+1 (866) 411-8655

ABOUT THE AUTHOR

JUDY CHATHAM

Judy Chatham is a lifelong student, teacher, wife, mother and grandmother. Writing prose and poetry have been both her avocation and her vocation. She has taught English Comp in grades 8-12 and in undergraduate freshman and sophomore classes. Her published writing began in the mid 1990s, first with a weekly news column, followed by four books of her own and three co-written books. For a decade she has led the local writing group, the Pen Pals who have published five books of their writings. Judy enjoys being from Indiana and has done extensive reading about Southern Indiana in the 1860-1940s era.

Printed in the USA
CPSIA information can be obtained
at www.ICGtesting.com
CBHW061459250624
10640CB00011B/63